BIRDWATCHING

NOTES

BIRDWATCHING

NOTES

CICO BOOKS
LONDON NEW YORK

Published in 2014 by CICO Books
an imprint of Ryland Peters & Small Ltd
20–21 Jockey's Fields, London WC1R 4BW
519 Broadway, 5th Floor, New York, NY 10012

www.rylandpeters.com

10 9 8 7 6 5 4 3 2 1

Compilation © CICO Books 2014
Design © CICO Books 2014
All illustrations © CORBIS

A CIP catalog record for this book is available from the Library of
Congress and the British Library.

ISBN: 978-1-78249-117-0

Designer: Barbara Zuñiga

Printed in China

Page 1: American White Pelican
(*Pelecanus erythrorhynchos*)
Pages 2-3: Roseate Spoonbill
(*Platalea ajaja*)
Pages 4–5: Long-tailed Ducks
(*Clangula hyemalis*)

CONTENTS

GETTING STARTED

Yellow-crowned Night Heron
(Nyctanassa violacea)
Opposite: American Crow
(Corvus brachyrhynchos)

KEEPING A BIRDWATCHING JOURNAL

American Robin
(Turdus migratorius)

Whether you are a committed birder, watch birds from the comfort of your own home, or notice them when you are out and about and are keen to know more, keeping a journal to record what you see will certainly enrich the experience. As well as the date, time, and location, make a note of anything that makes the sighting special. Suggestions for things to look out for and record include:

Appearance and behavior:

- Size, plumage, distinctive markings, bill shape, size, and color
- Is your bird on the ground or perching—among vegetation, on fencing or a building, or in flight? Note its flight patterns.
- Any head or tail bobbing, wing stretches? Is it displaying to attract a mate?
- Note foraging behavior.
- Note territorial behavior.
- Is it singing? Note bird song and any other sounds, e.g. drumming, and record if possible.
- Is the bird by itself or with others—of the same or a different species? Is it in a flock?

Habitat and weather conditions:

- How hot or cold is it?
- Is it bright or overcast?

- Are you watching in woodland, at the coast, near grassland, in an open or built-up area? Even if open, are there any buildings, e.g. a barn, in the vicinity?
- Note the type of vegetation in the immediate area.
- Are you near a river or stream?
- Also note how long you see the bird for and whether you have a clear view. Sightings can often be fleeting, so if you don't manage to observe everything, or write it down right away, don't worry. Jot down the information as soon as you can, and you will soon get to know the most important things to note.

EQUIPMENT SUGGESTIONS:

Binoculars (8 x 32)

Field guide to identification

Pen/pencil

Camera and sound recorder (perhaps on cell phone)

Waterproof clothing/footwear

Art supplies, if you want to sketch what you see

Note: Set cell phones to silent (or switch off) while you are watching birds if you don't want to scare them away—and earn the ire of fellow birders.

Slender-billed Curlew
(Numenius tenuirostris)

9

GRASSLAND BIRDS

Brewer's Blackbird *(Euphagus cyanocephalus)*
Opposite: top; Brown-headed Cowbird *(Molothrus ater)*;
bottom; Eastern Meadowlark *(Sturnella magna)*

Allan Brooks

Allen Brooks

GRASSLAND BIRDS

Spotted:

Where I was:

Date:

Special features:

Spotted:

Where I was:

Date:

Special features:

Spotted:

Where I was:

Date:

Special features:

Spotted:

Where I was:

Date:

Special features:

Spotted:

Where I was:

Date:

Special features:

Oregon Junco (*Junco hyemalis montanus*)

Spotted:

Where I was:

Date:

Special features:

American Tree
Sparrow
(Spizella arborea)

Spotted:

Where I was:

Date:

Special features:

Spotted:

Where I was:

Date:

Special features:

Spotted:

Where I was:

Date:

Special features:

Spotted:

Where I was:

Date:

Special features:

13

GRASSLAND BIRDS

Spotted:
....
Where I was:
....
Date:
....
Special features:
....
....

Spotted:
....
Where I was:
....
Date:
....
Special features:
....

Spotted:
....
Where I was:
....
Date:
....
Special features:
....

Brown-headed
Cowbird
(Molothrus ater)

Spotted:
....
Where I was:
....
Date:
....
Special features:
....

Spotted:
....
Where I was:
....
Date:
....
Special features:
....

Spotted:

Where I was:

Date:

Special features:

Spotted:

Where I was:

Date:

Special features:

Spotted:

Where I was:

Date:

Special features:

Brown-headed
Cowbird
(Molothrus ater)

Spotted:

Where I was:

Date:

Special features:

Spotted:

Where I was:

Date:

Special features:

GRASSLAND BIRDS

Spotted:

Where I was:

Date:

Special features:

Rough-legged
Hawk
(Buteo lagopus)

Spotted:

Where I was:

Date:

Special features:

Spotted:

Where I was:

Date:

Special features:

Spotted:

Where I was:

Date:

Special features:

Spotted:

Where I was:

Date:

Special features:

Spotted:

Where I was:

Date:

Special features:

Spotted:

Where I was:

Date:

Special features:

Spotted:

Where I was:

Date:

Special features:

Spotted:

Where I was:

Date:

Special features:

Spotted:

Where I was:

Date:

Special features:

Corn Bunting *(Emberiza calandra)*

GRASSLAND BIRDS

Spotted:

Where I was:

Date:

Special features:

Spotted:

Where I was:

Date:

Special features:

Eastern
Meadowlark
(Sturnella magna)

Spotted:

Where I was:

Date:

Special features:

Spotted:

Where I was:

Date:

Special features:

Spotted:

Where I was:

Date:

Special features:

Spotted:

Where I was:

Date:

Special features:

Spotted:

Where I was:

Date:

Special features:

L–R: Common
Reed Bunting
(Emberiza schoeniclus);
Lapland Longspur
(Calcarius lapponicus)

Spotted:

Where I was:

Date:

Special features:

Spotted:

Where I was:

Date:

Special features:

Spotted:

Where I was:

Date:

Special features:

GRASSLAND BIRDS

Spotted:

Where I was:

Date:

Special features:

Spotted:

Where I was:

Date:

Special features:

Spotted:

Where I was:

Date:

Special features:

Spotted:

Where I was:

Date:

Special features:

Spotted:

Where I was:

Date:

Special features:

Oregon Junco
(Junco hyemalis montanus)

Spotted:

Where I was:

Date:

Special features:

Rough-legged
Hawk
(Buteo lagopus)

Spotted:

Where I was:

Date:

Special features:

Spotted:

Where I was:

Date:

Special features:

Spotted:

Where I was:

Date:

Special features:

Spotted:

Where I was:

Date:

Special features:

GRASSLAND BIRDS

Spotted:

Where I was:

Date:

Special features:

Spotted:

Where I was:

Date:

Special features:

American Tree
Sparrow
(Spizella arborea)

Spotted:

Where I was:

Date:

Special features:

Spotted:

Where I was:

Date:

Special features:

Spotted:

Where I was:

Date:

Special features:

Spotted:

Where I was:

Date:

Special features:

Spotted:

Where I was:

Date:

Special features:

Spotted:

Where I was:

Date:

Special features:

Brown-headed
Cowbird
(Molothrus ater)

Spotted:

Where I was:

Date:

Special features:

Spotted:

Where I was:

Date:

Special features:

GRASSLAND BIRDS

Rough-legged Hawk
(Buteo lagopus)

Spotted:

Where I was:

Date:

Special features:

Spotted:

Where I was:

Date:

Special features:

Spotted:

Where I was:

Date:

Special features:

Spotted:

Where I was:

Date:

Special features:

Spotted:

Where I was:

Date:

Special features:

Spotted:

Where I was:

Date:

Special features:

Spotted:

Where I was:

Date:

Special features:

Spotted:

Where I was:

Date:

Special features:

Spotted:

Where I was:

Date:

Special features:

Spotted:

Where I was:

Date:

Special features:

Corn Bunting *(Emberiza calandra)*

GRASSLAND BIRDS

Spotted:

Where I was:

Date:

Special features:

Spotted:

Where I was:

Date:

Special features:

Spotted:

Where I was:

Date:

Special features:

Eastern
Meadowlark
(Sturnella magna)

Spotted:

Where I was:

Date:

Special features:

Spotted:

Where I was:

Date:

Special features:

Spotted:

Where I was:

Date:

Special features:

Spotted:

Where I was:

Date:

Special features:

Spotted:

Where I was:

Date:

Special features:

Oregon Junco
*(Junco hyemalis
montanus)*

Spotted:

Where I was:

Date:

Special features:

Spotted:

Where I was:

Date:

Special features:

GRASSLAND BIRDS

Spotted:

Where I was:

Date:

Special features:

Spotted:

Where I was:

Date:

Special features:

Spotted:

Where I was:

Date:

Special features:

Spotted:

Where I was:

Date:

Special features:

Spotted:

Where I was:

Date:

Special features:

L–R: Common Reed Bunting *(Emberiza schoeniclus)*; Lapland Longspur *(Calcarius lapponicus)*

Spotted:

Where I was:

Date:

Special features:

Rough-legged
Hawk
(Buteo lagopus)

Spotted:

Where I was:

Date:

Special features:

Spotted:

Where I was:

Date:

Special features:

Spotted:

Where I was:

Date:

Special features:

Spotted:

Where I was:

Date:

Special features:

GRASSLAND BIRDS

Spotted:

Where I was:

Date:

Special features:

Spotted:

Where I was:

Date:

Special features:

Spotted:

Where I was:

Date:

Special features:

Song Sparrow
(Melospiza melodia)

Spotted:

Where I was:

Date:

Special features:

Spotted:

Where I was:

Date:

Special features:

Spotted:

Where I was:

Date:

Special features:

Spotted:

Where I was:

Date:

Special features:

American Tree
Sparrow
(*Spizella arborea*)

Spotted:

Where I was:

Date:

Special features:

Spotted:

Where I was:

Date:

Special features:

Spotted:

Where I was:

Date:

Special features:

SHRUBLAND BIRDS

Song Sparrow *(Melospiza melodia)*
opposite: various species of
buntings, and, *center,* a Lapland
Longspur *(Calcarius lapponicus)*

SHRUBLAND BIRDS

Spotted:

Where I was:

Date:

Special features:

Spotted:

Where I was:

Date:

Special features:

Spotted:

Where I was:

Date:

Special features:

Spotted:

Where I was:

Date:

Special features:

Spotted:

Where I was:

Date:

Special features:

Blue Grosbeak *(Passerina caerulea)*

Blue Grosbeak
(Passerina caerulea)

Spotted:

Where I was:

Date:

Special features:

Spotted:

Where I was:

Date:

Special features:

Spotted:

Where I was:

Date:

Special features:

Spotted:

Where I was:

Date:

Special features:

Spotted:

Where I was:

Date:

Special features:

SHRUBLAND BIRDS

Spotted:

Where I was:

Date:

Special features:

Spotted:

Where I was:

Date:

Special features:

Oregon Junco
(*Junco hyemalis
montanus*)

Spotted:

Where I was:

Date:

Special features:

Spotted:

Where I was:

Date:

Special features:

Spotted:

Where I was:

Date:

Special features:

Spotted:

Where I was:

Date:

Special features:

Spotted:

Where I was:

Date:

Special features:

Spotted:

Where I was:

Date:

Special features:

Song Sparrow
(Melospiza melodia)

Spotted:

Where I was:

Date:

Special features:

Spotted:

Where I was:

Date:

Special features:

SHRUBLAND BIRDS

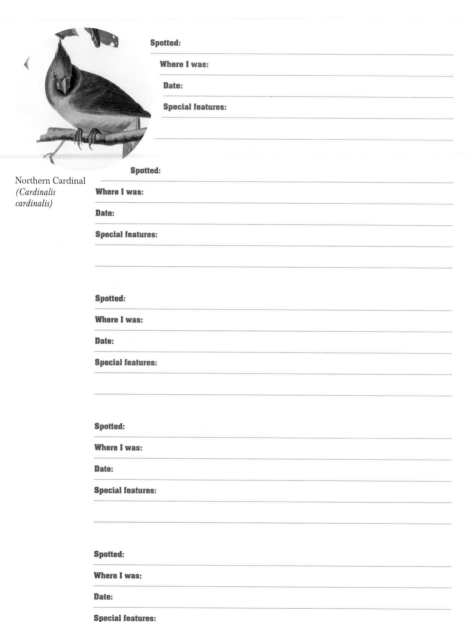

Spotted:

Where I was:

Date:

Special features:

Northern Cardinal
(Cardinalis cardinalis)

Spotted:

Where I was:

Date:

Special features:

Spotted:

Where I was:

Date:

Special features:

Spotted:

Where I was:

Date:

Special features:

Spotted:

Where I was:

Date:

Special features:

Spotted:

Where I was:

Date:

Special features:

Spotted:

Where I was:

Date:

Special features:

Spotted:

Where I was:

Date:

Special features:

Spotted:

Where I was:

Date:

Special features:

Spotted:

Where I was:

Date:

Special features:

Northern Cardinal
(Cardinalis cardinalis)

SHRUBLAND BIRDS

Spotted:

Where I was:

Date:

Special features:

Spotted:

Where I was:

Date:

Special features:

Spotted:

Where I was:

Date:

Special features:

Corn Bunting
(Emberiza calandra)

Spotted:

Where I was:

Date:

Special features:

Spotted:

Where I was:

Date:

Special features:

Spotted:

Where I was:

Date:

Special features:

Spotted:

Where I was:

Date:

Special features:

Spotted:

Where I was:

Date:

Special features:

Eastern Towhee
*(Pipilo
erythrophthalmus)*

Spotted:

Where I was:

Date:

Special features:

Spotted:

Where I was:

Date:

Special features:

41

SHRUBLAND BIRDS

Spotted:

Where I was:

Date:

Special features:

Spotted:

Where I was:

Date:

Special features:

Spotted:

Where I was:

Date:

Special features:

Spotted:

Where I was:

Date:

Special features:

Spotted:

Where I was:

Date:

Special features:

Indigo Bunting *(Passerina cyanea)*

Spotted:

Where I was:

Date:

Special features:

Indigo Bunting
(Passerina cyanea)

Spotted:

Where I was:

Date:

Special features:

Spotted:

Where I was:

Date:

Special features:

Spotted:

Where I was:

Date:

Special features:

Spotted:

Where I was:

Date:

Special features:

SHRUBLAND BIRDS

Spotted:

Where I was:

Date:

Special features:

Spotted:

Where I was:

Date:

Special features:

Spotted:

Where I was:

Date:

Special features:

Blue Grosbeak
(Passerina caerulea)

Spotted:

Where I was:

Date:

Special features:

Spotted:

Where I was:

Date:

Special features:

Spotted:

Where I was:

Date:

Special features:

Spotted:

Where I was:

Date:

Special features:

Spotted:

Where I was:

Date:

Special features:

Blue Grosbeak
(Passerina caerulea)

Spotted:

Where I was:

Date:

Special features:

Spotted:

Where I was:

Date:

Special features:

SHRUBLAND BIRDS

Eastern Towhee
(Pipilo erythrophthalmus)

Spotted:

Where I was:

Date:

Special features:

Spotted:

Where I was:

Date:

Special features:

Spotted:

Where I was:

Date:

Special features:

Spotted:

Where I was:

Date:

Special features:

Spotted:

Where I was:

Date:

Special features:

Spotted:

Where I was:

Date:

Special features:

Spotted:

Where I was:

Date:

Special features:

Spotted:

Where I was:

Date:

Special features:

Spotted:

Where I was:

Date:

Special features:

Spotted:

Where I was:

Date:

Special features:

Eastern Towhee
(Pipilo erythrophthalmus)

SHRUBLAND BIRDS

Spotted:

Where I was:

Date:

Special features:

Spotted:

Where I was:

Date:

Special features:

Spotted:

Where I was:

Date:

Special features:

Northern Cardinal
*(Cardinalis
cardinalis)*

Spotted:

Where I was:

Date:

Special features:

Spotted:

Where I was:

Date:

Special features:

Spotted:

Where I was:

Date:

Special features:

Spotted:

Where I was:

Date:

Special features:

Spotted:

Where I was:

Date:

Special features:

Northern Cardinal
*(Cardinalis
cardinalis)*

Spotted:

Where I was:

Date:

Special features:

Spotted:

Where I was:

Date:

Special features:

SHRUBLAND BIRDS

Spotted:

Where I was:

Date:

Special features:

Spotted:

Where I was:

Date:

Special features:

Spotted:

Where I was:

Date:

Special features:

Spotted:

Where I was:

Date:

Special features:

Spotted:

Where I was:

Date:

Special features:

L–R: Lapland Longspur *(Calcarius lapponicus)*; Common Reed Bunting *(Emberiza schoeniclus)*

Spotted:

Where I was:

Date:

Special features:

Snow Bunting
*(Plectrophenax
nivalis)*

Spotted:

Where I was:

Date:

Special features:

Spotted:

Where I was:

Date:

Special features:

Spotted:

Where I was:

Date:

Special features:

Spotted:

Where I was:

Date:

Special features:

SHRUBLAND BIRDS

Spotted:

Where I was:

Date:

Special features:

Spotted:

Where I was:

Date:

Special features:

Spotted:

Where I was:

Date:

Special features:

Cedar Waxwing
(Bombycilla cedrorum)

Spotted:

Where I was:

Date:

Special features:

Spotted:

Where I was:

Date:

Special features:

Spotted:

Where I was:

Date:

Special features:

Spotted:

Where I was:

Date:

Special features:

Spotted:

Where I was:

Date:

Special features:

Cedar Waxwing
(Bombycilla cedrorum)

Spotted:

Where I was:

Date:

Special features:

Spotted:

Where I was:

Date:

Special features:

WOODLAND BIRDS

Winter Wren *(Troglodytes hiemalis)*
Opposite: Pileated Woodpecker *(Dryocopus pileatus)*

WOODLAND BIRDS

Spotted:

Where I was:

Date:

Special features:

Spotted:

Where I was:

Date:

Special features:

Spotted:

Where I was:

Date:

Special features:

Spotted:

Where I was:

Date:

Special features:

Spotted:

Where I was:

Date:

Special features:

Western Tanager *(Piranga ludoviciana)*

Spotted:

Where I was:

Date:

Special features:

Western Tanager
(Piranga ludoviciana)

Spotted:

Where I was:

Date:

Special features:

Spotted:

Where I was:

Date:

Special features:

Spotted:

Where I was:

Date:

Special features:

Spotted:

Where I was:

Date:

Special features:

WOODLAND BIRDS

Spotted:

Where I was:

Date:

Special features:

Spotted:

Where I was:

Date:

Special features:

Pileated
Woodpecker
(Dryocopus pileatus)

Spotted:

Where I was:

Date:

Special features:

Spotted:

Where I was:

Date:

Special features:

Spotted:

Where I was:

Date:

Special features:

Spotted:

Where I was:

Date:

Special features:

Spotted:

Where I was:

Date:

Special features:

Spotted:

Where I was:

Date:

Special features:

Cedar Waxwing
(Bombycilla cedrorum)

Spotted:

Where I was:

Date:

Special features:

Spotted:

Where I was:

Date:

Special features:

WOODLAND BIRDS

Black-throated
Green Warbler
(Setophaga virens)

Spotted:

Where I was:

Date:

Special features:

Spotted:

Where I was:

Date:

Special features:

Spotted:

Where I was:

Date:

Special features:

Spotted:

Where I was:

Date:

Special features:

Spotted:

Where I was:

Date:

Special features:

Spotted:

Where I was:

Date:

Special features:

Spotted:

Where I was:

Date:

Special features:

Spotted:

Where I was:

Date:

Special features:

Spotted:

Where I was:

Date:

Special features:

Spotted:

Where I was:

Date:

Special features:

Black-throated Green Warbler *(Setophaga virens)*

WOODLAND BIRDS

Spotted:

Where I was:

Date:

Special features:

Spotted:

Where I was:

Date:

Special features:

Spotted:

Where I was:

Date:

Special features:

Black-billed
Cuckoo
*(Coccyzus
erythropthalmus)*

Spotted:

Where I was:

Date:

Special features:

Spotted:

Where I was:

Date:

Special features:

Spotted:

Where I was:

Date:

Special features:

Spotted:

Where I was:

Date:

Special features:

Spotted:

Where I was:

Date:

Special features:

Black-billed
Cuckoo
*(Coccyzus
erythropthalmus)*

Spotted:

Where I was:

Date:

Special features:

Spotted:

Where I was:

Date:

Special features:

WOODLAND BIRDS

Spotted:

Where I was:

Date:

Special features:

Spotted:

Where I was:

Date:

Special features:

Spotted:

Where I was:

Date:

Special features:

Spotted:

Where I was:

Date:

Special features:

Spotted:

Where I was:

Date:

Special features:

Eastern Whip-poor-will *(Antrostomus vociferus)*

Spotted:

Where I was:

Date:

Special features:

Winter Wren
(Troglodytes hiemalis)

Spotted:

Where I was:

Date:

Special features:

Spotted:

Where I was:

Date:

Special features:

Spotted:

Where I was:

Date:

Special features:

Spotted:

Where I was:

Date:

Special features:

WOODLAND BIRDS

Spotted:

Where I was:

Date:

Special features:

Spotted:

Where I was:

Date:

Special features:

Spotted:

Where I was:

Date:

Special features:

Cedar Waxwing
(Bombycilla cedrorum)

Spotted:

Where I was:

Date:

Special features:

Spotted:

Where I was:

Date:

Special features:

Spotted:

Where I was:

Date:

Special features:

Spotted:

Where I was:

Date:

Special features:

Spotted:

Where I was:

Date:

Special features:

Cedar Waxwing
(Bombycilla cedrorum)

Spotted:

Where I was:

Date:

Special features:

Spotted:

Where I was:

Date:

Special features:

WOODLAND BIRDS

Eastern Whip-poor-will
(Antrostomus vociferus)

Spotted:

Where I was:

Date:

Special features:

Spotted:

Where I was:

Date:

Special features:

Spotted:

Where I was:

Date:

Special features:

Spotted:

Where I was:

Date:

Special features:

Spotted:

Where I was:

Date:

Special features:

Spotted:
....

Where I was:
....

Date:
....

Special features:
....

....

Spotted:
....

Where I was:
....

Date:
....

Special features:
....

....

Spotted:
....

Where I was:
....

Date:
....

Special features:
....

....

Spotted:
....

Where I was:
....

Date:
....

Special features:
....

....

Spotted:
....

Where I was:
....

Date:
....

Special features:
....

....

Eastern Whip-poor-will *(Antrostomus vociferus)*

WOODLAND BIRDS

Spotted:

Where I was:

Date:

Special features:

Spotted:

Where I was:

Date:

Special features:

Spotted:

Where I was:

Date:

Special features:

Western Tanager
(Piranga ludoviciana)

Spotted:

Where I was:

Date:

Special features:

Spotted:

Where I was:

Date:

Special features:

Spotted:

Where I was:

Date:

Special features:

Spotted:

Where I was:

Date:

Special features:

Spotted:

Where I was:

Date:

Special features:

Western Tanager
(Piranga ludoviciana)

Spotted:

Where I was:

Date:

Special features:

Spotted:

Where I was:

Date:

Special features:

WOODLAND BIRDS

Spotted:

Where I was:

Date:

Special features:

Spotted:

Where I was:

Date:

Special features:

Spotted:

Where I was:

Date:

Special features:

Spotted:

Where I was:

Date:

Special features:

Spotted:

Where I was:

Date:

Special features:

Black-throated Green Warbler *(Setophaga virens)*

Spotted:

Where I was:

Date:

Special features:

Winter Wren
(Troglodytes hiemalis)

Spotted:

Where I was:

Date:

Special features:

Spotted:

Where I was:

Date:

Special features:

Spotted:

Where I was:

Date:

Special features:

Spotted:

Where I was:

Date:

Special features:

WOODLAND BIRDS

Spotted:

Where I was:

Date:

Special features:

Spotted:

Where I was:

Date:

Special features:

Spotted:

Where I was:

Date:

Special features:

Black-billed
Cuckoo
*(Coccyzus
erythropthalmus)*

Spotted:

Where I was:

Date:

Special features:

Spotted:

Where I was:

Date:

Special features:

Spotted:

Where I was:

Date:

Special features:

Spotted:

Where I was:

Date:

Special features:

Spotted:

Where I was:

Date:

Special features:

Pileated
Woodpecker
(*Dryocopus pileatus*)

Spotted:

Where I was:

Date:

Special features:

Spotted:

Where I was:

Date:

Special features:

WATER BIRDS

Yellow-crowned Night Heron *(Nyctanassa violacea)*
Opposite: Mallard Duck *(Anas platyrhynchos)*

WATER BIRDS

Spotted:

Where I was:

Date:

Special features:

Spotted:

Where I was:

Date:

Special features:

Spotted:

Where I was:

Date:

Special features:

Spotted:

Where I was:

Date:

Special features:

Spotted:

Where I was:

Date:

Special features:

American White Pelican *(Pelecanus erythrorhynchos)*

Spotted:

Where I was:

Date:

Special features:

Slender-billed
Curlew
*(Numenius
tenuirostris)*

Spotted:

Where I was:

Date:

Special features:

Spotted:

Where I was:

Date:

Special features:

Spotted:

Where I was:

Date:

Special features:

Spotted:

Where I was:

Date:

Special features:

WATER BIRDS

Spotted:

Where I was:

Date:

Special features:

Spotted:

Where I was:

Date:

Special features:

Spotted:

Where I was:

Date:

Special features:

Black-throated
Loon
(Gavia arctica)

Spotted:

Where I was:

Date:

Special features:

Spotted:

Where I was:

Date:

Special features:

Spotted:

Where I was:

Date:

Special features:

Spotted:

Where I was:

Date:

Special features:

Spotted:

Where I was:

Date:

Special features:

Black-throated
Loon
(*Gavia arctica*)

Spotted:

Where I was:

Date:

Special features:

Spotted:

Where I was:

Date:

Special features:

WATER BIRDS

Spotted:

Where I was:

Date:

Special features:

Long-tailed Ducks
(Clangula hyemalis)

Spotted:

Where I was:

Date:

Special features:

Spotted:

Where I was:

Date:

Special features:

Spotted:

Where I was:

Date:

Special features:

Spotted:

Where I was:

Date:

Special features:

Spotted:
....

Where I was:
....

Date:
....

Special features:
....

....

Spotted:
....

Where I was:
....

Date:
....

Special features:
....

....

Spotted:
....

Where I was:
....

Date:
....

Special features:
....

....

Spotted:
....

Where I was:
....

Date:
....

Special features:
....

....

Spotted:
....

Where I was:
....

Date:
....

Special features:
....

....

Long-tailed Ducks *(Clangula hyemalis)*

WATER BIRDS

Spotted:

Where I was:

Date:

Special features:

Spotted:

Where I was:

Date:

Special features:

Spotted:

Where I was:

Date:

Special features:

L–R: Kentish Plover
*(Charadrius
alexandrinus)*;
Snowy Plover
(Charadrius nivosus);
Piping Plover
(Charadrius melodus)

Spotted:

Where I was:

Date:

Special features:

Spotted:

Where I was:

Date:

Special features:

Spotted:

Where I was:

Date:

Special features:

Spotted:

Where I was:

Date:

Special features:

Spotted:

Where I was:

Date:

Special features:

Ringed Plovers
(Charadrius hiaticula)

Spotted:

Where I was:

Date:

Special features:

Spotted:

Where I was:

Date:

Special features:

WATER BIRDS

Spotted:

Where I was:

Date:

Special features:

Spotted:

Where I was:

Date:

Special features:

Spotted:

Where I was:

Date:

Special features:

Spotted:

Where I was:

Date:

Special features:

Spotted:

Where I was:

Date:

Special features:

Atlantic Puffin *(Fratercula arctica)*

Spotted:

Where I was:

Date:

Special features:

Black Guillemot
(Cepphus grylle)

Spotted:

Where I was:

Date:

Special features:

Spotted:

Where I was:

Date:

Special features:

Spotted:

Where I was:

Date:

Special features:

Spotted:

Where I was:

Date:

Special features:

WATER BIRDS

Spotted:

Where I was:

Date:

Special features:

Spotted:

Where I was:

Date:

Special features:

Spotted:

Where I was:

Date:

Special features:

Yellow-crowned
Night Heron
*(Nyctanassa
violacea)*

Spotted:

Where I was:

Date:

Special features:

Spotted:

Where I was:

Date:

Special features:

Spotted:

Where I was:

Date:

Special features:

Spotted:

Where I was:

Date:

Special features:

Spotted:

Where I was:

Date:

Special features:

Slender-billed
Curlew
*(Numenius
tenuirostris)*

Spotted:

Where I was:

Date:

Special features:

Spotted:

Where I was:

Date:

Special features:

WATER BIRDS

Western Sandpipers *(Calidris)*

Spotted:

Where I was:

Date:

Special features:

Spotted:

Where I was:

Date:

Special features:

Spotted:

Where I was:

Date:

Special features:

Spotted:

Where I was:

Date:

Special features:

Spotted:

Where I was:

Date:

Special features:

Spotted:

Where I was:

Date:

Special features:

Spotted:

Where I was:

Date:

Special features:

Spotted:

Where I was:

Date:

Special features:

Spotted:

Where I was:

Date:

Special features:

Spotted:

Where I was:

Date:

Special features:

Mallard Duck *(Anas platyrhynchos)*

WATER BIRDS

Spotted:

Where I was:

Date:

Special features:

Spotted:

Where I was:

Date:

Special features:

American White
Pelican *(Pelecanus
erythrorhynchos)*

Spotted:

Where I was:

Date:

Special features:

Spotted:

Where I was:

Date:

Special features:

Spotted:

Where I was:

Date:

Special features:

Spotted:

Where I was:

Date:

Special features:

Spotted:

Where I was:

Date:

Special features:

Spotted:

Where I was:

Date:

Special features:

Yellow-crowned
Night Heron
(Nyctanassa violacea)

Spotted:

Where I was:

Date:

Special features:

Spotted:

Where I was:

Date:

Special features:

WATER BIRDS

Spotted:

Where I was:

Date:

Special features:

Spotted:

Where I was:

Date:

Special features:

Spotted:

Where I was:

Date:

Special features:

Spotted:

Where I was:

Date:

Special features:

Spotted:

Where I was:

Date:

Special features:

Yellow-crowned Night Heron *(Nyctanassa violacea)*

Spotted:

Where I was:

Date:

Special features:

Black Guillemots
(Cepphus grylle)

Spotted:

Where I was:

Date:

Special features:

Spotted:

Where I was:

Date:

Special features:

Spotted:

Where I was:

Date:

Special features:

Spotted:

Where I was:

Date:

Special features:

WATER BIRDS

Spotted:

Where I was:

Date:

Special features:

Spotted:

Where I was:

Date:

Special features:

Red Knot
(Calidris canutus)

Spotted:

Where I was:

Date:

Special features:

Spotted:

Where I was:

Date:

Special features:

Spotted:

Where I was:

Date:

Special features:

Spotted:

Where I was:

Date:

Special features:

Spotted:

Where I was:

Date:

Special features:

Spotted:

Where I was:

Date:

Special features:

Yellow-crowned
Night Heron
(Nyctanassa violacea)

Spotted:

Where I was:

Date:

Special features:

Spotted:

Where I was:

Date:

Special features:

URBAN BIRDS

House Sparrow *(Passer domesticus)*
Opposite: Trumpeter Swan *(Cygnus buccinator)*

URBAN BIRDS

Spotted:

Where I was:

Date:

Special features:

Spotted:

Where I was:

Date:

Special features:

Spotted:

Where I was:

Date:

Special features:

Spotted:

Where I was:

Date:

Special features:

Spotted:

Where I was:

Date:

Special features:

American Robin *(Turdus migratorius)*

Spotted: ....

Where I was: ....

Date: ....

Special features: ....

....

Mallard Duck
(Anas platyrhynchos)

Spotted: ....

Where I was: ....

Date: ....

Special features: ....

....

Spotted: ....

Where I was: ....

Date: ....

Special features: ....

....

Spotted: ....

Where I was: ....

Date: ....

Special features: ....

....

Spotted: ....

Where I was: ....

Date: ....

Special features: ....

....

URBAN BIRDS

Spotted:
....

Where I was:
....

Date:
....

Special features:
....
....
....

Spotted:
....

Where I was:
....

Date:
....

Special features:
....

Spotted:
....

Where I was:
....

Date:
....

Special features:
....

House Sparrow
(Passer domesticus)

Spotted:
....

Where I was:
....

Date:
....

Special features:
....
....

Spotted:
....

Where I was:
....

Date:
....

Special features:
....
....

Spotted:

Where I was:

Date:

Special features:

Spotted:

Where I was:

Date:

Special features:

Spotted:

Where I was:

Date:

Special features:

House Finch
*(Haemorhous
mexicanus)*

Spotted:

Where I was:

Date:

Special features:

Spotted:

Where I was:

Date:

Special features:

URBAN BIRDS

Spotted:

Where I was:

Date:

Special features:

American Robin
(Turdus migratorius)

Spotted:

Where I was:

Date:

Special features:

Spotted:

Where I was:

Date:

Special features:

Spotted:

Where I was:

Date:

Special features:

Spotted:

Where I was:

Date:

Special features:

Spotted:

Where I was:

Date:

Special features:

Spotted:

Where I was:

Date:

Special features:

Spotted:

Where I was:

Date:

Special features:

Spotted:

Where I was:

Date:

Special features:

Spotted:

Where I was:

Date:

Special features:

Mallard Duck *(Anas platyrhynchos)*

URBAN BIRDS

Spotted:

Where I was:

Date:

Special features:

Spotted:

Where I was:

Date:

Special features:

Spotted:

Where I was:

Date:

Special features:

House Finch
(*Haemorhous mexicanus*)

Spotted:

Where I was:

Date:

Special features:

Spotted:

Where I was:

Date:

Special features:

Spotted:

Where I was:

Date:

Special features:

Spotted:

Where I was:

Date:

Special features:

Spotted:

Where I was:

Date:

Special features:

Trumpeter Swan
(Cygnus buccinator)

Spotted:

Where I was:

Date:

Special features:

Spotted:

Where I was:

Date:

Special features:

URBAN BIRDS

Spotted:

Where I was:

Date:

Special features:

Spotted:

Where I was:

Date:

Special features:

Spotted:

Where I was:

Date:

Special features:

Spotted:

Where I was:

Date:

Special features:

Spotted:

Where I was:

Date:

Special features:

House Sparrow *(Passer domesticus)*

Spotted:

Where I was:

Date:

Special features:

American Crow
(Corvus brachyrhynchos)

Spotted:

Where I was:

Date:

Special features:

Spotted:

Where I was:

Date:

Special features:

Spotted:

Where I was:

Date:

Special features:

Spotted:

Where I was:

Date:

Special features:

URBAN BIRDS

Spotted:

Where I was:

Date:

Special features:

Spotted:

Where I was:

Date:

Special features:

Spotted:

Where I was:

Date:

Special features:

American Robin
(Turdus migratorius)

Spotted:

Where I was:

Date:

Special features:

Spotted:

Where I was:

Date:

Special features:

Spotted:

Where I was:

Date:

Special features:

Spotted:

Where I was:

Date:

Special features:

Spotted:

Where I was:

Date:

Special features:

Redwing
(Turdus iliacus)

Spotted:

Where I was:

Date:

Special features:

Spotted:

Where I was:

Date:

Special features:

URBAN BIRDS

Mallard Duck
(Anas platyrhynchos)

Spotted:

Where I was:

Date:

Special features:

Spotted:

Where I was:

Date:

Special features:

Spotted:

Where I was:

Date:

Special features:

Spotted:

Where I was:

Date:

Special features:

Spotted:

Where I was:

Date:

Special features:

Spotted:

Where I was:

Date:

Special features:

Spotted:

Where I was:

Date:

Special features:

Spotted:

Where I was:

Date:

Special features:

Spotted:

Where I was:

Date:

Special features:

Spotted:

Where I was:

Date:

Special features:

House Sparrow *(Passer domesticus)*

URBAN BIRDS

Spotted:

Where I was:

Date:

Special features:

Spotted:

Where I was:

Date:

Special features:

Spotted:

Where I was:

Date:

Special features:

Mallard Duck
(Anas platyrhynchos)

Spotted:

Where I was:

Date:

Special features:

Spotted:

Where I was:

Date:

Special features:

Spotted:

Where I was:

Date:

Special features:

Spotted:

Where I was:

Date:

Special features:

Spotted:

Where I was:

Date:

Special features:

Trumpeter Swan
(Cygnus buccinator)

Spotted:

Where I was:

Date:

Special features:

Spotted:

Where I was:

Date:

Special features:

URBAN BIRDS

Spotted:

Where I was:

Date:

Special features:

Spotted:

Where I was:

Date:

Special features:

Spotted:

Where I was:

Date:

Special features:

Spotted:

Where I was:

Date:

Special features:

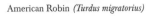

Spotted:

Where I was:

Date:

Special features:

American Robin *(Turdus migratorius)*

Spotted:
....

Where I was:
....

Date:
....

Special features:
....
....

House Sparrow
(Passer domesticus)

Spotted:
....

Where I was:
....

Date:
....

Special features:
....
....

Spotted:
....

Where I was:
....

Date:
....

Special features:
....
....

Spotted:
....

Where I was:
....

Date:
....

Special features:
....
....

Spotted:
....

Where I was:
....

Date:
....

Special features:
....
....

URBAN BIRDS

Spotted:

Where I was:

Date:

Special features:

Spotted:

Where I was:

Date:

Special features:

Spotted:

Where I was:

Date:

Special features:

Redwing
(Turdus iliacus)

Spotted:

Where I was:

Date:

Special features:

Spotted:

Where I was:

Date:

Special features:

Spotted:

Where I was:

Date:

Special features:

Spotted:

Where I was:

Date:

Special features:

Spotted:

Where I was:

Date:

Special features:

House Finch
*(Haemorhous
mexicanus)*

Spotted:

Where I was:

Date:

Special features:

Spotted:

Where I was:

Date:

Special features:

FAVORITE PLACES
TO SEE BIRDS

American Robin *(Turdus migratorius)*
Opposite: King Eider *(Somateria spectabilis)*

KING DUCK, *Male 1, Female 2.*

FAVORITE PLACES TO SEE BIRDS

Location:

Date visited:

Species seen:

Notes:

Location:

Date visited:

Species seen:

Notes:

Location:

Date visited:

Species seen:

Notes:

Location:

Date visited:

Species seen:

Notes:

Location:

Date visited:

Species seen:

Notes:

Red Knot *(Calidris canutus)*

Location:

Date visited:

Species seen:

Notes:

Brewer's Blackbird
*(Euphagus
cyanocephalus)*

Location:

Date visited:

Species seen:

Notes:

Location:

Date visited:

Species seen:

Notes:

Location:

Date visited:

Species seen:

Notes:

Location:

Date visited:

Species seen:

Notes:

FAVORITE PLACES TO SEE BIRDS

Location:

Date visited:

Species seen:

Notes:

Location:

Date visited:

Species seen:

Notes:

Location:

Date visited:

Species seen:

Notes:

L–R: Lapland
Longspur
*(Calcarius
lapponicus)*;
Common Reed
Bunting
*(Emberiza
schoeniclus)*

Location:

Date visited:

Species seen:

Notes:

Location:

Date visited:

Species seen:

Notes:

Location:

Date visited:

Species seen:

Notes:

Location:

Date visited:

Species seen:

Notes:

Location:

Date visited:

Species seen:

Notes:

Eastern
Meadowlark
(Sturnella magna)

Location:

Date visited:

Species seen:

Notes:

Location:

Date visited:

Species seen:

Notes:

FAVORITE PLACES TO SEE BIRDS

Blue Grosbeak
(Passerina caerulea)

Location:

Date visited:

Species seen:

Notes:

Location:

Date visited:

Species seen:

Notes:

Location:

Date visited:

Species seen:

Notes:

Location:

Date visited:

Species seen:

Notes:

Location:

Date visited:

Species seen:

Notes:

Location:

Date visited:

Species seen:

Notes:

Location:

Date visited:

Species seen:

Notes:

Location:

Date visited:

Species seen:

Notes:

Location:

Date visited:

Species seen:

Notes:

Location:

Date visited:

Species seen:

Notes:

Blue Grosbeak *(Passerina caerulea)*

FAVORITE PLACES TO SEE BIRDS

Location:

Date visited:

Species seen:

Notes:

Location:

Date visited:

Species seen:

Notes:

Snow Bunting
(Plectrophenax nivalis)

Location:

Date visited:

Species seen:

Notes:

Location:

Date visited:

Species seen:

Notes:

Location:

Date visited:

Species seen:

Notes:

Location: ....

Date visited: ....

Species seen: ....

Notes: ....

....

....

Location: ....

Date visited: ....

Species seen: ....

Notes: ....

....

Red-tailed Hawk
(Buteo jamaicensis)

Location: ....

Date visited: ....

Species seen: ....

Notes: ....

....

Location: ....

Date visited: ....

Species seen: ....

Notes: ....

....

....

Location: ....

Date visited: ....

Species seen: ....

Notes: ....

....

FAVORITE PLACES TO SEE BIRDS

Location:

Date visited:

Species seen:

Notes:

Location:

Date visited:

Species seen:

Notes:

Location:

Date visited:

Species seen:

Notes:

Location:

Date visited:

Species seen:

Notes:

Location:

Date visited:

Species seen:

Notes:

Northern Cardinal *(Cardinalis cardinalis)*

Location:

Date visited:

Species seen:

Notes:

Northern Cardinal
(Cardinalis cardinalis)

Location:

Date visited:

Species seen:

Notes:

Location:

Date visited:

Species seen:

Notes:

Location:

Date visited:

Species seen:

Notes:

Location:

Date visited:

Species seen:

Notes:

FAVORITE PLACES TO SEE BIRDS

Location:

Date visited:

Species seen:

Notes:

Location:

Date visited:

Species seen:

Notes:

Eastern Whip-
poor-will
*(Antrostomus
vociferus)*

Location:

Date visited:

Species seen:

Notes:

Location:

Date visited:

Species seen:

Notes:

Location:

Date visited:

Species seen:

Notes:

Location:

Date visited:

Species seen:

Notes:

Location:

Date visited:

Species seen:

Notes:

Location:

Date visited:

Species seen:

Notes:

Song Sparrow
(Melospiza melodia)

Location:

Date visited:

Species seen:

Notes:

Location:

Date visited:

Species seen:

Notes:

FAVORITE PLACES TO SEE BIRDS

King Eider
*(Somateria
spectabilis)*

Location:

Date visited:

Species seen:

Notes:

Location:

Date visited:

Species seen:

Notes:

Location:

Date visited:

Species seen:

Notes:

Location:

Date visited:

Species seen:

Notes:

Location:

Date visited:

Species seen:

Notes:

Location:

Date visited:

Species seen:

Notes:

Location:

Date visited:

Species seen:

Notes:

Location:

Date visited:

Species seen:

Notes:

Location:

Date visited:

Species seen:

Notes:

Location:

Date visited:

Species seen:

Notes:

Corn Bunting *(Emberiza calandra)*

FAVORITE PLACES TO SEE BIRDS

Location:

Date visited:

Species seen:

Notes:

Location:

Date visited:

Species seen:

Notes:

Indigo Bunting
(Passerina cyanea)

Location:

Date visited:

Species seen:

Notes:

Location:

Date visited:

Species seen:

Notes:

Location:

Date visited:

Species seen:

Notes:

Location: ....

Date visited: ....

Species seen: ....

Notes: ....

....

Location: ....

Date visited: ....

Species seen: ....

Notes: ....

....

Location: ....

Date visited: ....

Species seen: ....

Notes: ....

....

Pileated
Woodpecker
(*Dryocopus pileatus*)

Location: ....

Date visited: ....

Species seen: ....

Notes: ....

....

Location: ....

Date visited: ....

Species seen: ....

Notes: ....

....

FAVORITE PLACES TO SEE BIRDS

Location:

Date visited:

Species seen:

Notes:

Location:

Date visited:

Species seen:

Notes:

Location:

Date visited:

Species seen:

Notes:

Location:

Date visited:

Species seen:

Notes:

Location:

Date visited:

Species seen:

Notes:

Western Tanager *(Piranga ludoviciana)*

Location:

Date visited:

Species seen:

Notes:

Slender-billed
Curlew
*(Numenius
tenuirostris)*

Location:

Date visited:

Species seen:

Notes:

Location:

Date visited:

Species seen:

Notes:

Location:

Date visited:

Species seen:

Notes:

Location:

Date visited:

Species seen:

Notes:

FAVORITE PLACES TO SEE BIRDS

Location:

Date visited:

Species seen:

Notes:

Location:

Date visited:

Species seen:

Notes:

Brown-headed
Cowbird
(Molothrus ater)

Location:

Date visited:

Species seen:

Notes:

Location:

Date visited:

Species seen:

Notes:

Location:

Date visited:

Species seen:

Notes:

Location:

Date visited:

Species seen:

Notes:

Location:

Date visited:

Species seen:

Notes:

Location:

Date visited:

Species seen:

Notes:

House Finch
(*Haemorhous mexicanus*)

Location:

Date visited:

Species seen:

Notes:

Location:

Date visited:

Species seen:

Notes:

KEEPING ORGANIZED

Western Tanager *(Piranga ludoviciana)*
Opposite: American Flamingo *(Phoenicopterus ruber)*

BIRD FAIRS VISITED

Location:

Date visited:

Species seen:

Notes:

Location:

Date visited:

Species seen:

Notes:

Location:

Date visited:

Species seen:

Notes:

Location:

Date visited:

Species seen:

Notes:

Location:

Date visited:

Species seen:

Notes:

Northern Cardinal *(Cardinalis cardinalis)*

Location:

Date visited:

Species seen:

Notes:

Western Tanager
*(Piranga
ludoviciana)*

Location:

Date visited:

Species seen:

Notes:

Location:

Date visited:

Species seen:

Notes:

Location:

Date visited:

Species seen:

Notes:

Location:

Date visited:

Species seen:

Notes:

BIRD FAIRS VISITED

Location:

Date visited:

Species seen:

Notes:

Location:

Date visited:

Species seen:

Notes:

Red-tailed Hawk
(Buteo jamaicensis)

Location:

Date visited:

Species seen:

Notes:

Location:

Date visited:

Species seen:

Notes:

Location:

Date visited:

Species seen:

Notes:

Location:

Date visited:

Species seen:

Notes:

Location:

Date visited:

Species seen:

Notes:

Location:

Date visited:

Species seen:

Notes:

Red-tailed Hawk
(Buteo jamaicensis)

Location:

Date visited:

Species seen:

Notes:

Location:

Date visited:

Species seen:

Notes:

BIRD FAIRS VISITED

American
Flamingo
*(Phoenicopterus
ruber)*

Location:

Date visited:

Species seen:

Notes:

Location:

Date visited:

Species seen:

Notes:

Location:

Date visited:

Species seen:

Notes:

Location:

Date visited:

Species seen:

Notes:

Location:

Date visited:

Species seen:

Notes:

Location:

Date visited:

Species seen:

Notes:

Location:

Date visited:

Species seen:

Notes:

Location:

Date visited:

Species seen:

Notes:

Location:

Date visited:

Species seen:

Notes:

Location:

Date visited:

Species seen:

Notes:

Winter Wren *(Troglodytes hiemalis)*

BIRD FAIRS VISITED

Location:

Date visited:

Species seen:

Notes:

Location:

Date visited:

Species seen:

Notes:

Long-tailed Ducks
(Clangula hyemalis)

Location:

Date visited:

Species seen:

Notes:

Location:

Date visited:

Species seen:

Notes:

Location:

Date visited:

Species seen:

Notes:

Location:

Date visited:

Species seen:

Notes:

Location:

Date visited:

Species seen:

Notes:

Location:

Date visited:

Species seen:

Notes:

Long-tailed Ducks
(Clangula hyemalis)

Location:

Date visited:

Species seen:

Notes:

Location:

Date visited:

Species seen:

Notes:

BIRD FAIRS VISITED

Location:

Date visited:

Species seen:

Notes:

Location:

Date visited:

Species seen:

Notes:

Location:

Date visited:

Species seen:

Notes:

Location:

Date visited:

Species seen:

Notes:

Location:

Date visited:

Species seen:

Notes:

Eastern Whip-poor-will *(Antrostomus vociferus)*

American Crow
(Corvus brachyrhynchos)

Location:

Date visited:

Species seen:

Notes:

Location:

Date visited:

Species seen:

Notes:

Location:

Date visited:

Species seen:

Notes:

Location:

Date visited:

Species seen:

Notes:

Location:

Date visited:

Species seen:

Notes:

BIRD RESERVATIONS VISITED

Location:

Date visited:

Species seen:

Notes:

Location:

Date visited:

Species seen:

Notes:

Eastern
Meadowlark
(Sturnella magna)

Location:

Date visited:

Species seen:

Notes:

Location:

Date visited:

Species seen:

Notes:

Location:

Date visited:

Species seen:

Notes:

Location:

Date visited:

Species seen:

Notes:

Location:

Date visited:

Species seen:

Notes:

Location:

Date visited:

Species seen:

Notes:

Brown-headed
Cowbird
(Molothrus ater)

Location:

Date visited:

Species seen:

Notes:

Location:

Date visited:

Species seen:

Notes:

BIRD RESERVATIONS VISITED

Location:

Date visited:

Species seen:

Notes:

Red Knot
(Calidris canutus)

Location:

Date visited:

Species seen:

Notes:

Location:

Date visited:

Species seen:

Notes:

Location:

Date visited:

Species seen:

Notes:

Location:

Date visited:

Species seen:

Notes:

Location:

Date visited:

Species seen:

Notes:

Location:

Date visited:

Species seen:

Notes:

Location:

Date visited:

Species seen:

Notes:

Location:

Date visited:

Species seen:

Notes:

Location:

Date visited:

Species seen:

Notes:

Western Sandpipers *(Calidris)*

BIRD RESERVATIONS VISITED

Location:

Date visited:

Species seen:

Notes:

Location:

Date visited:

Species seen:

Notes:

Yellow-crowned
Night Heron
(Nyctanassa violacea)

Location:

Date visited:

Species seen:

Notes:

Location:

Date visited:

Species seen:

Notes:

Location:

Date visited:

Species seen:

Notes:

Location:

Date visited:

Species seen:

Notes:

Location:

Date visited:

Species seen:

Notes:

Location:

Date visited:

Species seen:

Notes:

Yellow-crowned
Night Heron
(Nyctanassa violacea)

Location:

Date visited:

Species seen:

Notes:

Location:

Date visited:

Species seen:

Notes:

BIRD RESERVATIONS VISITED

Location:

Date visited:

Species seen:

Notes:

Location:

Date visited:

Species seen:

Notes:

Location:

Date visited:

Species seen:

Notes:

Location:

Date visited:

Species seen:

Notes:

Location:

Date visited:

Species seen:

Notes:

Pileated Woodpecker *(Dryocopus pileatus)*

Location: ....

Date visited: ....

Species seen: ....

Notes: ....

Corn Bunting
(Emberiza calandra)

Location: ....

Date visited: ....

Species seen: ....

Notes: ....

Location: ....

Date visited: ....

Species seen: ....

Notes: ....

Location: ....

Date visited: ....

Species seen: ....

Notes: ....

Location: ....

Date visited: ....

Species seen: ....

Notes: ....

BIRD RESERVATIONS VISITED

Location:

Date visited:

Species seen:

Notes:

Location:

Date visited:

Species seen:

Notes:

American Robin
(*Turdus migratorius*)

Location:

Date visited:

Species seen:

Notes:

Location:

Date visited:

Species seen:

Notes:

Location:

Date visited:

Species seen:

Notes:

Location:

Date visited:

Species seen:

Notes:

Location:

Date visited:

Species seen:

Notes:

Location:

Date visited:

Species seen:

Notes:

House Finch
*(Haemorhous
mexicanus)*

Location:

Date visited:

Species seen:

Notes:

Location:

Date visited:

Species seen:

Notes:

USEFUL WEBSITES

Use this space to jot down the addresses of websites you find useful

Mallard Duck *(Anas platyrhynchos)*

Black-billed
Cuckoo *(Coccyzus
erythropthalmus)*

NOTES

Northern Cardinal *(Cardinalis cardinalis)*

Western Tanager
(Piranga ludoviciana)

NOTES

Red-tailed Hawk
(Buteo jamaicensis)

Red-tailed Hawk
(Buteo jamaicensis)

NOTES

King Eider
*(Somateria
spectabilis)*

Red Knot *(Calidris canutus)*

NOTES

Long-tailed Ducks
(Clangula hyemalis)

Long-tailed Ducks
(Clangula hyemalis)

NOTES

Eastern Whip-poor-will *(Antrostomus vociferus)*

American Crow
(Corvus brachyrhynchos)

NOTES

King Eider
(Somateria spectabilis)

American
Flamingo
*(Phoenicopterus
ruber)*

NOTES

Slender-billed
Curlew
*(Numenius
tenuirostris)*

Western Sandpipers *(Calidris)*

SKETCHES

Yellow-crowned Night Heron
(Nyctanassa violacea)

House Finch *(Haemorhous mexicanus)*

SKETCHES

Pileated Woodpecker *(Dryocopus pileatus)*

American Tree Sparrow
(Spizella arborea)

183

SKETCHES

American Robin *(Turdus migratorius)*

Cedar Waxwing
(Bombycilla cedrorum)

SKETCHES

Mallard Duck *(Anas platyrhynchos)*

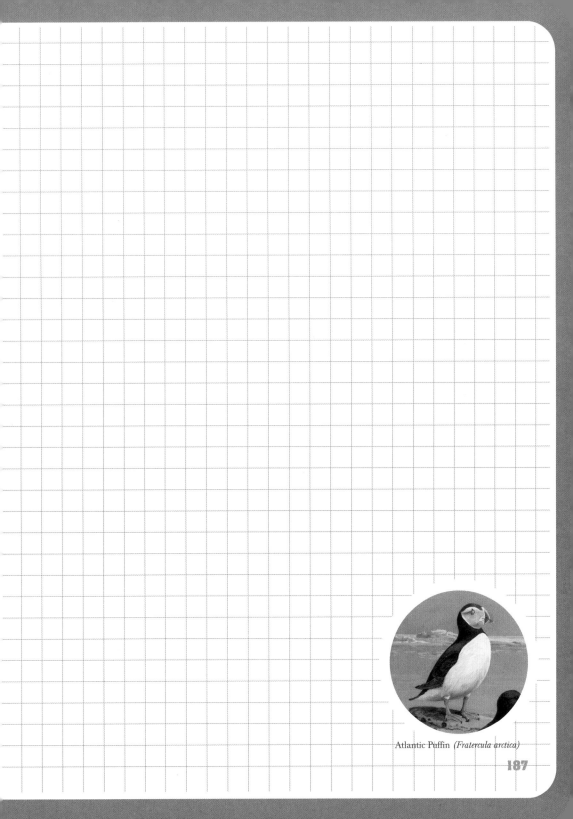

Atlantic Puffin *(Fratercula arctica)*

SKETCHES

Red-tailed Hawk *(Buteo jamaicensis)*

L–R: Common Reed Bunting
(Emberiza schoeniclus); Lapland
Longspur *(Calcarius lapponicus)*

SKETCHES

Brown-headed Cowbird *(Molothrus ater)*

Rough-legged Hawk
(Buteo lagopus)

191

SKETCHES

Black-throated Green Warbler
(Setophaga virens)